piano / vocal / g

CHRISTIAN CHART TOPPERS

ISBN 978-1-4234-9229-0

HAL•LEONARD®
CORPORATION
7777 W. BLUEMOUND RD. P.O. BOX 13819 MILWAUKEE, WI 53213

Visit Hal Leonard Online at
www.halleonard.com

ALL OF CREATION

Words and Music by MERCYME,
DAN MUCKALA and BROWN BANNISTER

Moderate Rock beat

Sep - a - rat - ed,

un - til the veil ___ was torn, ___ the mo - ment that hope ___

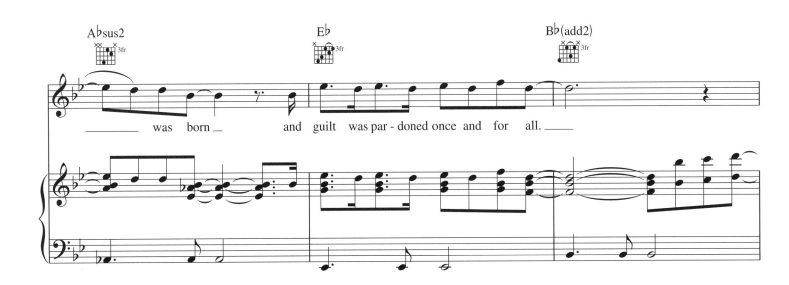

___ was born ___ and guilt was par - doned once and for all. ___

BEAUTIFUL ONE

Words and Music by
TIM HUGHES

Wonderful, so wonderful is Your unfailing love. Your
Powerful, so powerful, Your glory fills the sky, Your

BRAVE

Words by NICHOLE NORDEMAN
Music by NICHOLE NORDEMAN and JAY JOYCE

BRING THE RAIN

Words and Music by BART MILLARD, BARRY GRAUL,
JIM BRYSON, NATHAN COCHRAN,
MIKE SCHEUCHZER and ROBBY SHAFFER

cir - cum - stanc - es pos - si - bly__ change who I for - ev - er am__ in You?__

May - be since__ my life__ was changed__ long be - fore__ these rain - y days,__ it's
I am Yours__ re - gard - less of _____ the clouds__ that__ may loom__ a - bove,__ be -

CALL MY NAME

Words and Music by MAC POWELL,
DAVID CARR, TAI ANDERSON,
BRAD AVERY and MARK LEE

CRY OUT TO JESUS

Words by MAC POWELL
Music by MAC POWELL, DAVID CARR,
TAI ANDERSON, BRAD AVERY and MARK LEE

ev - er - y - one _____ who's lost _____ some - one they _____ love _____
mar - riage that's _____ strug - gl - ing _____ just _____ to hang _____ on, _____

To

DOES ANYBODY HEAR HER

Words and Music by
MARK HALL

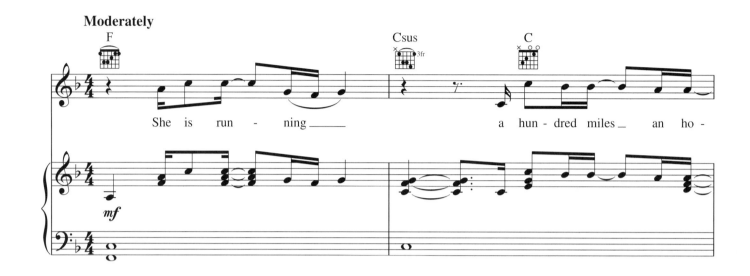

She is run- ning _____ a hun- dred miles_ an ho-

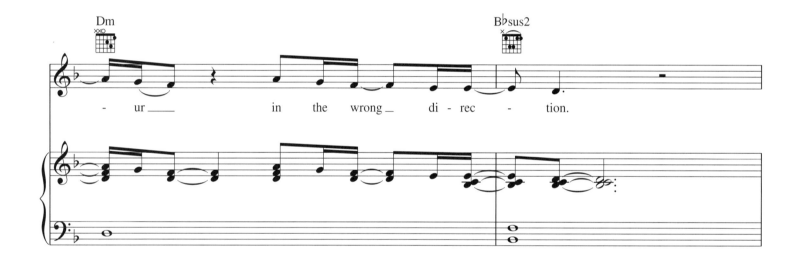

-ur _____ in the wrong_ di - rec - tion.

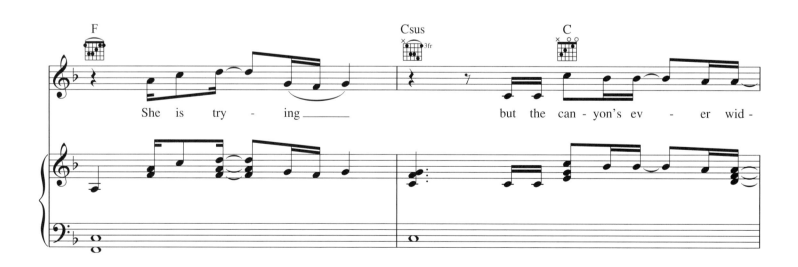

She is try- ing _____ but the can- yon's ev - er wid-

EAST TO WEST

Words and Music by MARK HALL
and BERNIE HERMS

Moderate Rock beat

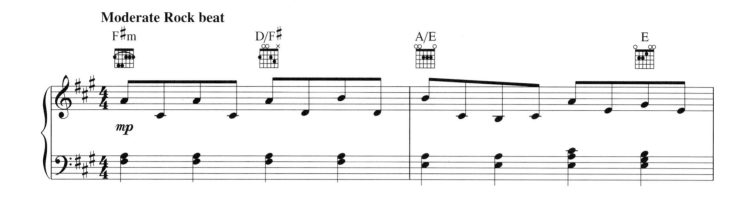

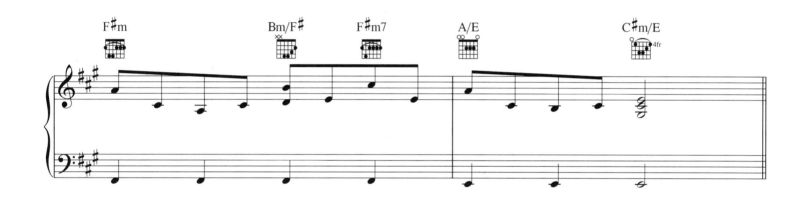

Here I am,__ Lord, and__ I'm drown - ing in Your sea of for - get - ful - ness.__

CITY ON OUR KNEES

Words and Music by TOBY McKEEHAN,
JAMES MOORE and CARY BARLOWE

EVERYTIME I BREATHE

Words and Music by MIKE WEAVER,
MICHAEL FARREN and ANDY CLONINGER

Moderately slow, in 2

FREE TO BE ME

Words and Music by
FRANCESCA BATTISTELLI

GIVE ME YOUR EYES

Words and Music by JASON INGRAM
and BRANDON HEATH

*Recorded a half step lower.

GLORY DEFINED

Words and Music by JIM COOPER,
KENNY LAMB and JASON ROY

Moderate Rock

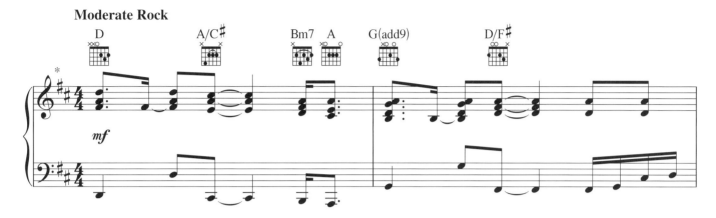

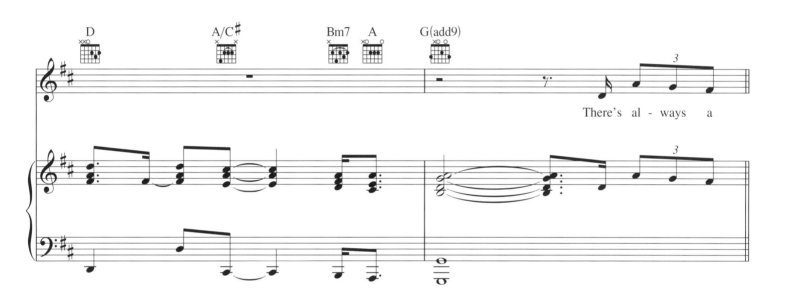

There's al-ways a

bet-ter way, ___ there's al-ways a bridge that needs ___ cross-ing, ___ there's al-ways the

* Recorded a half step lower.

cross o - ver Jor - dan, ___ I know that I'll ___ be run - ning home, ___ and I'll

know that I'll ___ be run - ning home ___ to You. ___

And I'll be run - ning home ___ to You. ___

GIVE THIS CHRISTMAS AWAY

Words and Music by MATTHEW WEST
and SAM MIZELL

GOD WITH US

Words and Music by BART MILLARD,
NATHAN COCHRAN, MIKE SCHEUCHZER,
JIM BRYSON, BARRY GRAUL
and ROBBY SHAFFER

Moderately

Who are we _____ that You would be

mind-ful of ___ us? What do You ___ see _____

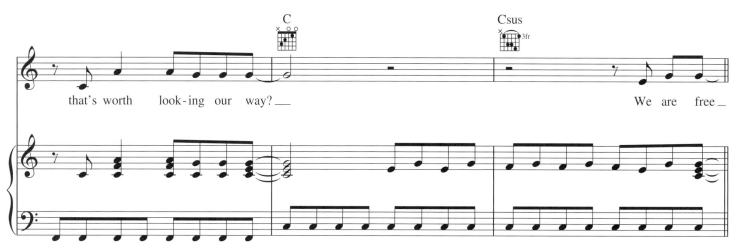

that's worth look-ing our way? ___ We are free ___

* Recorded a half step lower.

HERE WITH ME

Words and Music by BRAD RUSSELL,
BART MILLARD, MICHAEL SCHEUCHZER, JAMES BRYSON,
ROBIN SHAFFER, NATHAN COCHRAN, BARRY GRAUL,
DAN MUCKALA and PETE KIPLEY

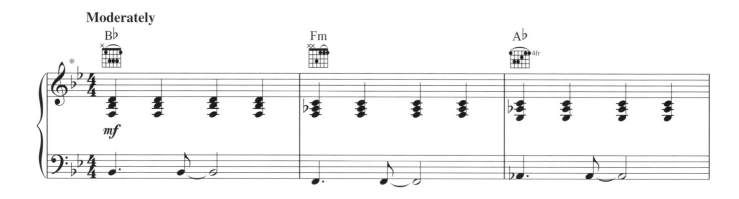

I long for Your em - brace ___

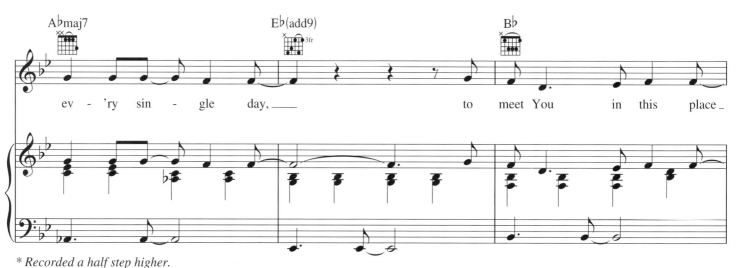

ev - 'ry sin - gle day, ___ to meet You in this place _

* Recorded a half step higher.

HIDE

Words and Music by MATTHEW WEST,
JASON HOUSER and JOY WILLIAMS

HOW GREAT IS OUR GOD

Words and Music by CHRIS TOMLIN,
JESSE REEVES and ED CASH

Recorded a half step lower.

I'M NOT WHO I WAS

Words and Music by
BRANDON HEATH

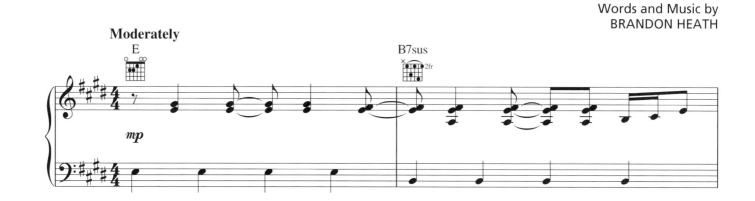

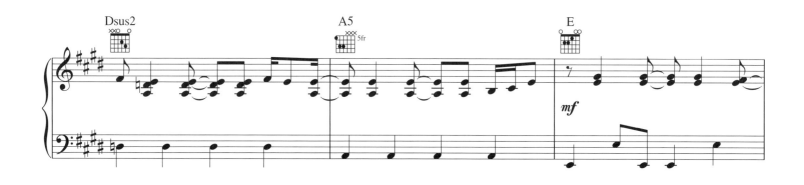

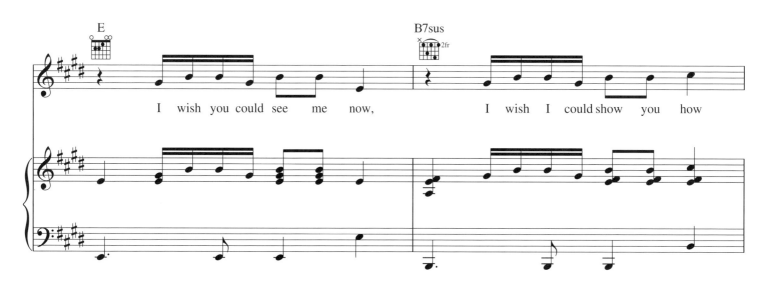

I wish you could see me now,   I wish I could show you how

but I nev-er got to tell you

so.

I found us in a pho-to-graph,

I saw me and I had to laugh. You know, I'm not who I

IN THE BLINK OF AN EYE

Words and Music by BART MILLARD,
NATHAN COCHRAN, MIKE SCHEUCHZER,
JIM BRYSON, ROBBY SHAFFER,
BARRY GRAUL and PETER KIPLEY

JOSEPH'S LULLABY

Words and Music by BART MILLARD
and BROWN BANNISTER

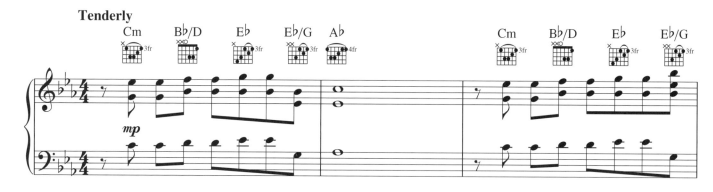

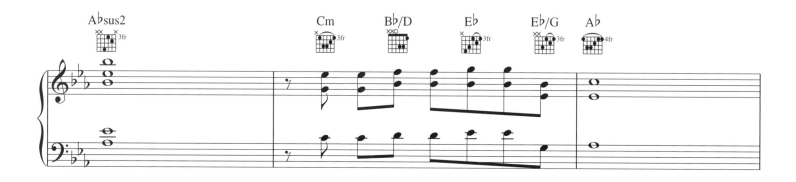

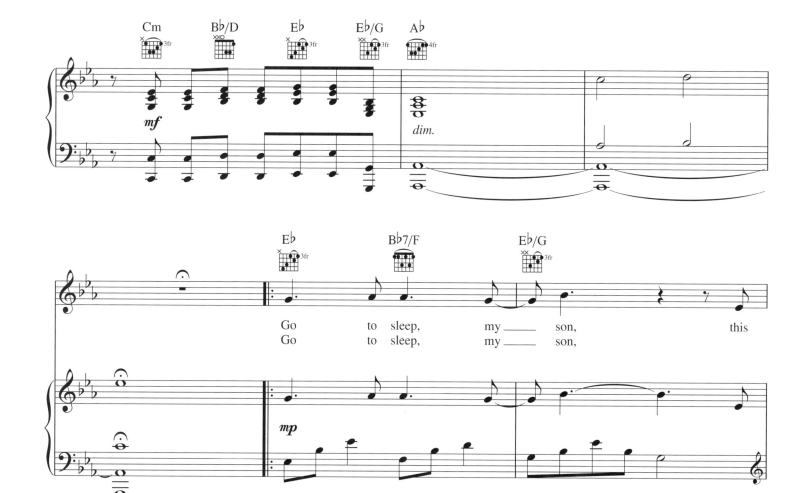

Go to sleep, my ____ son, this
Go to sleep, my ____ son,

LET IT FADE

Words and Music by JEREMY CAMP
and ADAM WATTS

Moderately, in 2

Have you been walk-ing on a sur-

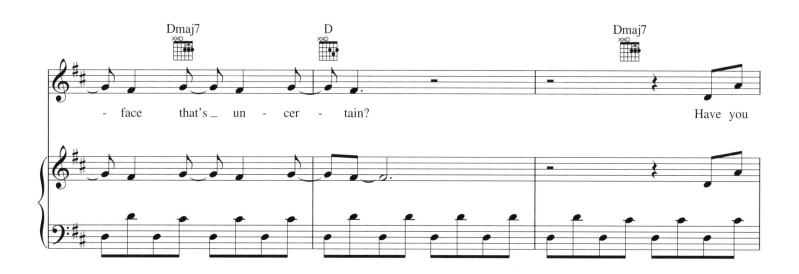

-face that's un-cer-tain? Have you

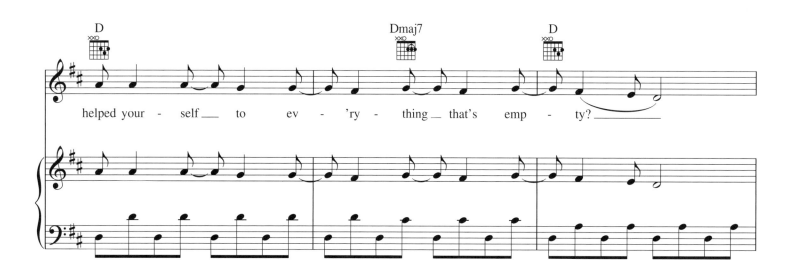

helped your-self to ev-'ry-thing that's emp-ty?

LIFESONG

Words and Music by
MARK HALL

* Recorded a half step higher.

MADE TO LOVE

Words and Music by TOBY McKEEHAN,
CARY BARLOWE, JAMIE MOORE
and AARON RICE

175

MORE

Words and Music by KENNY GREENBERG,
JASON HOUSER and MATTHEW WEST

MADE TO WORSHIP

Words and Music by CHRIS TOMLIN,
ED CASH and STEPHAN SHARP

Be-

fore the day, be - fore the light, __ be

All we are __ and all we have __ is

fore the world __ re - volved __ a - round __ the sun, ___

all a gift __ from God __ that we __ re - ceive. __

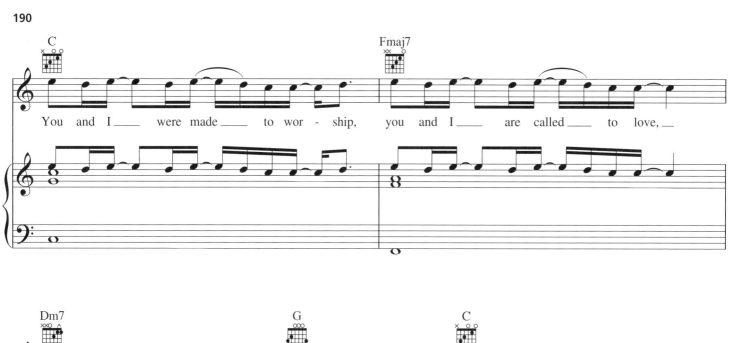

You and I ___ were made ___ to wor-ship, you and I ___ are called ___ to love, ___

you and I ___ are for-giv-en and free, ___ yeah. ___ When you and I ___ em-brace ___ sur-ren - der,

D.S. al Coda

you and I ___ choose to ___ be-lieve, _ then you and I will see, ___ you ___ and I ___ will see.

CODA

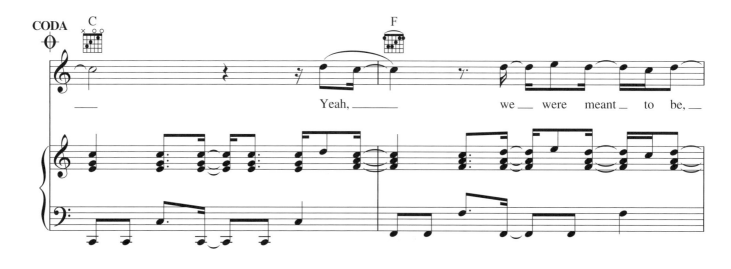

Yeah, _____ we ___ were meant ___ to be, ___

THE MOTIONS

Words and Music by SAM MIZELL,
MATTHEW WEST and JASON HOUSER

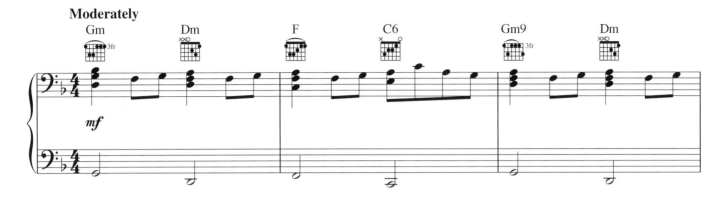

This might hurt, _ it's not safe, _
No re - grets, _ not this time. _

_ but I know that I've got - ta make _ a change. I don't care _ if I break; _
_ I'm gon - na let my _ heart de - feat _ my mind, let Your love _ make me whole. _

I don't wan - na go, I don't wan - na go _____ through the mo -

- tions. (Take me all the way.) ____

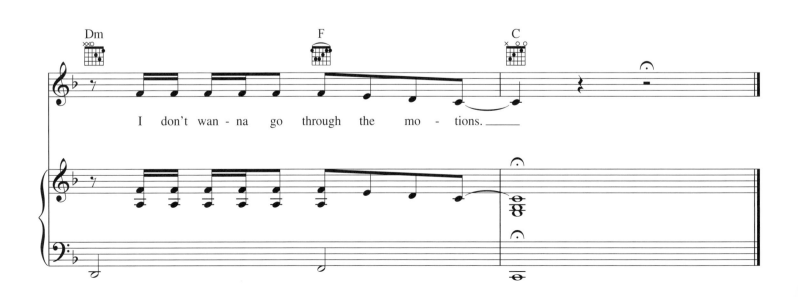

I don't wan - na go through the mo - tions. ____

MY SAVIOR MY GOD

Words and Music by
AARON SHUST

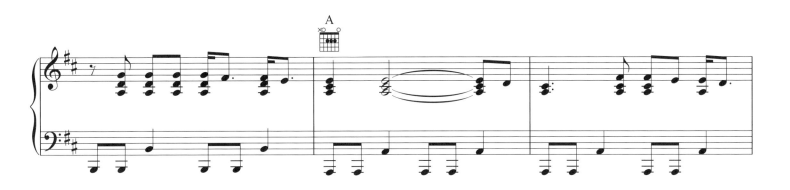

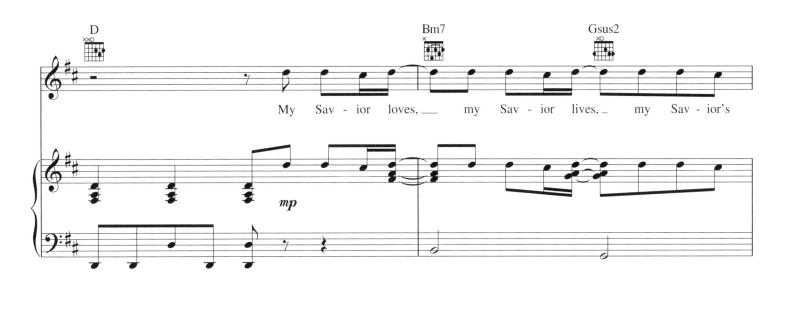

My Sav - ior loves, ___ my Sav - ior lives, ___ my Sav - ior's

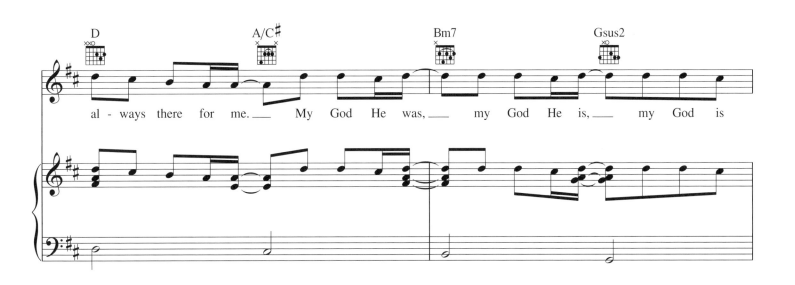

al - ways there for me. ___ My God He was, ___ my God He is, ___ my God is

MOUNTAIN OF GOD

Words and Music by MAC POWELL
and BROWN BANNISTER

Moderately slow

I thought that I _ was all _ a-lone, bro-ken and a-fraid, _ but You were _ there
as I trav-el on _ the road that You have led _ me down, _ You are _ here

_ with me. _ Yes, You were there _ with me. _
_ with me. _ Yes, You are here _ with me. _ And

And I did-n't e-ven know_ that I had lost _ my way, _ but You were _ there
I have need_ for noth-ing more,_ oh, now that I _ have found_ that You are _ here

O COME O COME EMMANUEL

Words and Music by
AARON SHUST

214

REVELATION SONG

Words and Music by
JENNIE LEE RIDDLE

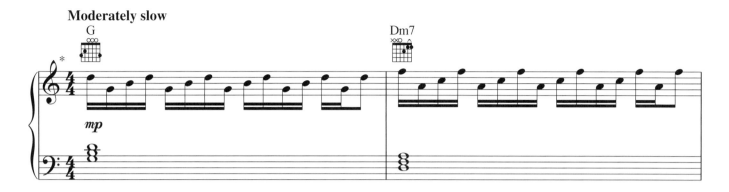

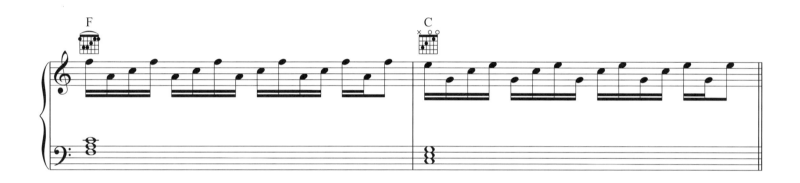

Wor-thy is the Lamb who was slain. Ho-ly, ho-ly is He.

Recorded a half step lower.

PRAISE YOU IN THIS STORM

Words and Music by MARK HALL
and BERNIE HERMS

Moderately slow

I was sure __ by now, ___ God, You would have __ reached down __
I re-mem-ber when __ I stum-bled in __ the wind. __

__ and wiped our tears ___ a - way, ___ stepped in and saved __
You heard my cry ___ to You, ___ and raised me up __

__ the day. __ But once a - gain __ I say, __ "A - men," __
__ a - gain. __ But my strength is al - most gone. __ How can I car - ry on __

*Recorded a half step higher.

I praise You in ___ this storm. ___

SING A SONG

Words and Music by MAC POWELL,
MARK LEE, BRAD AVERY,
TAI ANDERSON and DAVID CARR

Well, I wan-na sing_ a song_ for You,_ Lord. _____ And,

Lord, for You_ I want_ to sing_ a song. _____ And

I wan-na lift_ my voice_ to Heav - en _____ and

SO LONG SELF

Words and Music by BART MILLARD, BARRY GRAUL,
JIM BRYSON, NATHAN COCHRAN,
MIKE SCHEUCHZER and ROBBY SHAFFER

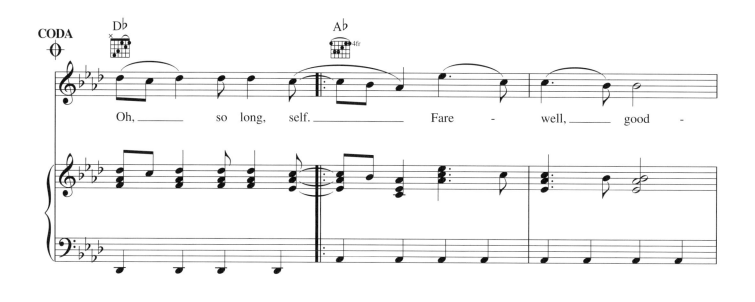

Oh,_____ so long, self._____ Fare - well,_____ good -

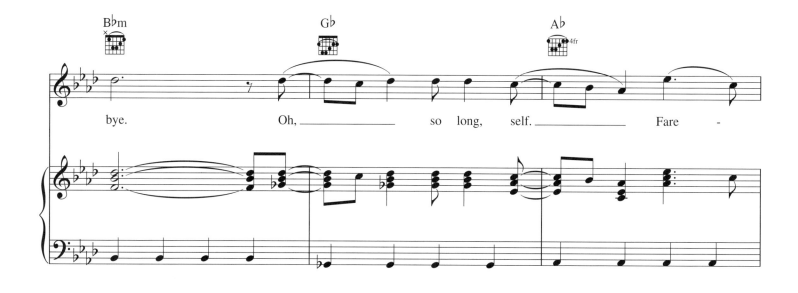

bye.   Oh,_____ so long, self._____ Fare -

TAKE YOU BACK

Words and Music by
JEREMY CAMP

THERE WILL BE A DAY

Words and Music by
JEREMY CAMP

Moderate Ballad

I try to hold__ on to__ this world__ with ev - 'ry-thing__ I have,__

__ but I feel__ the weight__ of what it brings and the hurt that tries__ to grab.__

* *Recorded a half step lower.*

THIS MAN

Words and Music by
JEREMY CAMP

UNDO

Words and Music by SCOTT DAVIS,
WES WILLIS and KEVIN HUGULEY

Moderate Rock beat

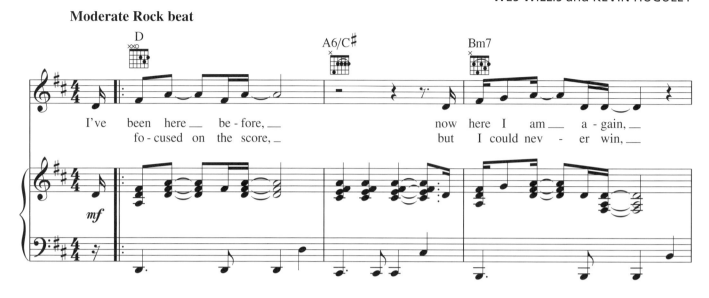

I've been here __ be-fore, __ now here I am a-gain, __
fo-cused on the score, __ but I could nev-er win, __

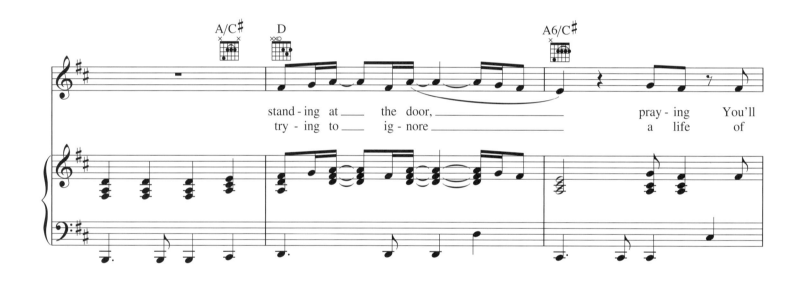

stand-ing at __ the door, __ pray-ing You'll
try-ing to __ ig-nore __ a life of

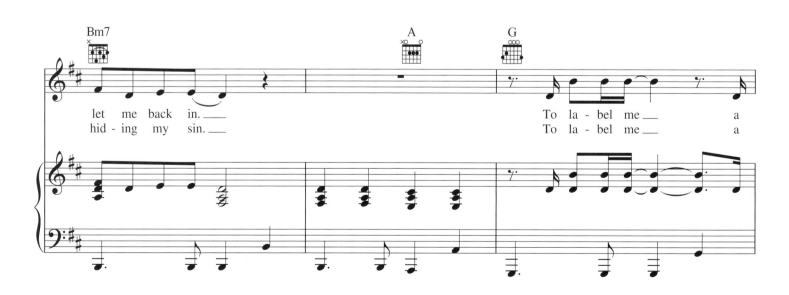

let me back in. __ To la-bel me __ a
hid-ing my sin. __ To la-bel me __ a

276

UNTIL THE WHOLE WORLD HEARS

Words and Music by MARK HALL,
ROGER GLIDEWELL, JASON McARTHUR
and BERNIE HERMS

Lord, I want to feel with Your heart____ and see the world thru Your eyes.____

Recorded a half step lower.

Ho - ly na - tions sanc - ti - fy, ___ let this be ___ our bat - tle cry. ___

sing un - til ___ the whole world ___ hears. ___

Whoa, _____ whoa. _____

VOICE OF TRUTH

Words and Music by MARK HALL
and STEVEN CURTIS CHAPMAN

WALK BY FAITH

Words and Music by
JEREMY CAMP

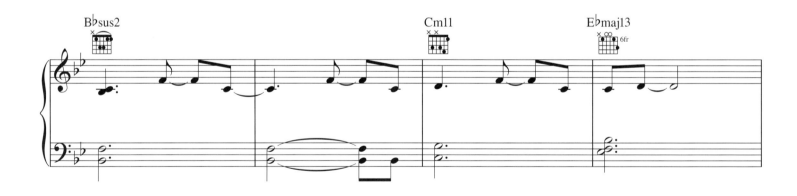

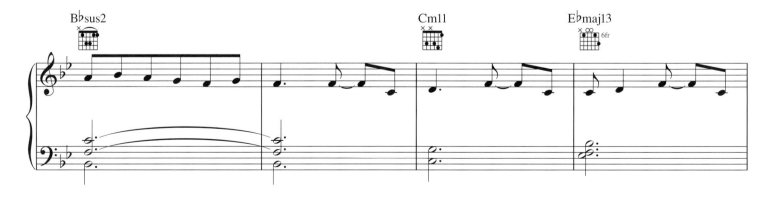

WASHED BY THE WATER

Words and Music by NATHANIEL RINEHART
and WILLIAM RINEHART

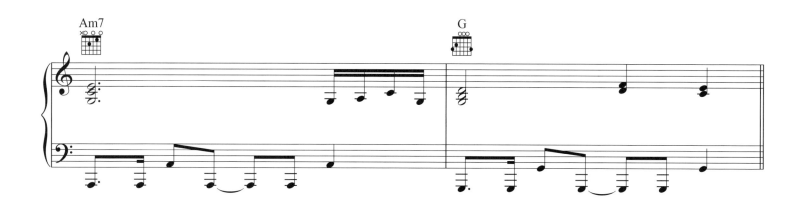

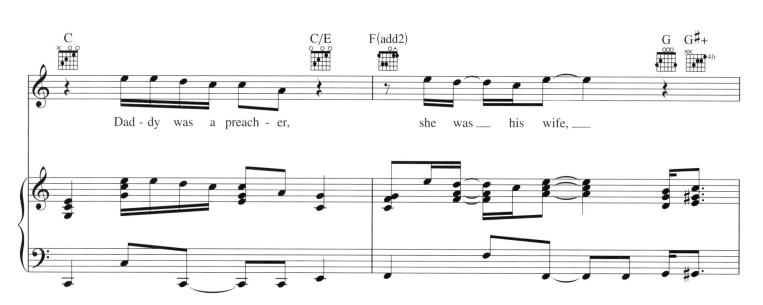

Recorded a half step lower.

WHO AM I

Words and Music by
MARK HALL

Who am I ____

that the Lord of all ____ the earth ____ would
that the eyes that see ____ my sin ____ would

care to know ____ my name, ____ would care to feel ____ my hurt?
look on me ____ with love ____ and watch me rise ____ a-gain?

Recorded a half step higher.

Not be - cause of who __ I am, ____ but be -

cause of what __ You've done. ____ Not be - cause of what __ I've done, __

WORD OF GOD SPEAK

Words and Music by BART MILLARD
and PETE KIPLEY

YOU ARE EVERYTHING

Words and Music by MATTHEW WEST
and SAM MIZELL

With joy, in a slow 2

I'm the one with two left feet, ___ stand-ing on a lone-ly street.

I can't e - ven walk a straight line. And

To Coda

feel - ing all this life with - in, ev - 'ry sin - gle beat of my ___ heart. ___

I'm the one with big mis - takes, big re - grets and big - ger breaks than

F
can't be - lieve is hap - pen - ing. You're stand - ing right in front of me with
E♭
3fr
arms wide o - pen. All I know is, ev - 'ry day is filled with hope 'cause
B♭
Gm7
You are ev - 'ry - thing that I breathe for,
Fsus
and I can't help but breathe You in and breathe a - gain,

YOU ARE MY KING
(Amazing Love)

Words and Music by
BILLY JAMES FOOTE

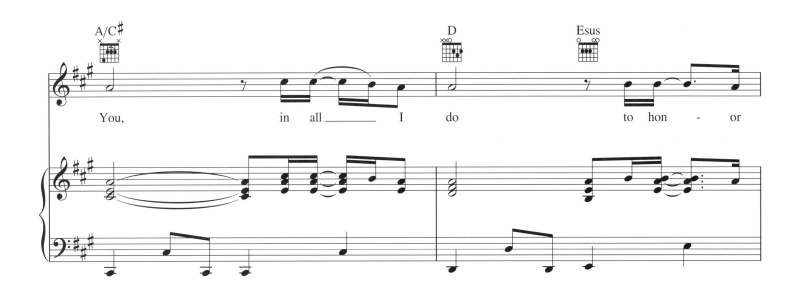

WHAT FAITH CAN DO

Words and Music by SCOTT DAVIS
and SCOTT KRIPPAYNE

YOU ARE SO GOOD TO ME

Words and Music by DON CHAFFER,
BEN PASLEY and ROBIN PASLEY

Moderate Rock

Well, You are beau-ti-ful,__ my sweet, sweet song._____ You are

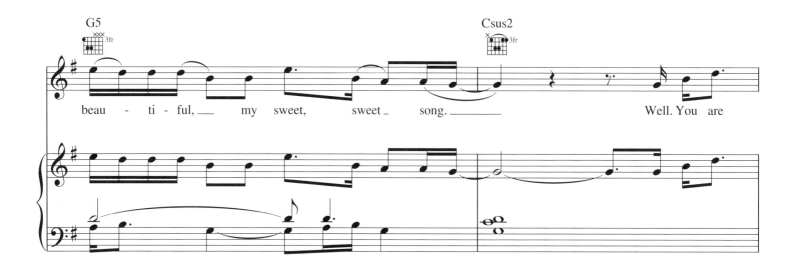

beau-ti-ful,__ my sweet, sweet__ song._____ Well. You are

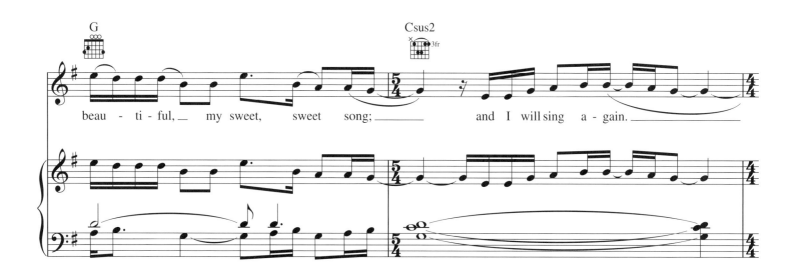

beau-ti-ful,__ my sweet, sweet song;_____ and I will sing a-gain.__

THE BEST OF CONTEMPORARY CHRISTIAN MUSIC

The ancient Greek "sign of the fish" (Ichthys) is an instantly recognizable Christian symbol in pop culture. It is used on car bumpers, clothing, jewelry, business logos, and more. Hal Leonard is proud to offer The Fish Series, showcasing the wide variety of music styles that comprise the Contemporary Christian genre. From the early pioneers of CCM to today's biggest hits, there's something for everyone!

CHRISTMAS (Green Book)
40 Contemporary Christian holiday favorites, including: Christmas Angels • Christmas Is All in the Heart • He Made a Way in a Manger • Joseph's Lullaby • Manger Throne • Not That Far from Bethlehem • 2000 Decembers Ago • While You Were Sleeping • and more.
00311755 P/V/G...................................$19.95

PRAISE (Yellow Book)
50 songs of praise and worship, including: Agnus Dei • Before the Throne of God Above • Come Just As You Are • He Knows My Name • Majesty • Open Our Eyes • Worthy of Worship • You Are My All in All • and many more.
00311759 P/V/G...................................$19.99

EARLY YEARS (Orange Book)
41 songs, including: The Day He Wore My Crown • Father's Eyes • I Wish We'd All Been Ready • Love Crucified Arose • Rise Again • Sing Your Praise to the Lord • Who Will Save the Children • Your Love Broke Through • and more.
00311756 P/V/G...................................$19.99

ROCK (Black Book)
41 rock hits from some of the biggest names in Contemporary Christian music, including: All Around Me • Count Me In • Everlasting God • I'm Not Alright • Meant to Live • No Matter What It Takes • Tunnel • Undo • and more.
00311760 P/V/G...................................$19.95

INSPIRATIONAL (Blue Book)
42 songs of encouragement and exaltation, including: Call on Jesus • Find Your Wings • God Will Make a Way • Healing Rain • Jesus Will Still Be There • On My Knees • Say the Name • Your Grace Still Amazes Me • and many more.
00311757 P/V/G...................................$19.95

WEDDING (White Book)
40 songs from Contemporary Christian artists for the bride and groom's big day, including: Cinderella • God Knew That I Needed You • Household of Faith • I Will Be Here • Look What Love Has Done • A Page Is Turned • This Day • Without Love • and more.
00311761 P/V/G...................................$19.99

POP (Red Book)
44 top pop hits from favorite Contemporary Christian artists, including: Always Have, Always Will • Brave • Circle of Friends • For Future Generations • If We Are the Body • Simple Things • To Ever Live Without Me • What It Means • and more.
00311758 P/V/G...................................$21.95

WORSHIP (Purple Book)
50 songs perfect for a worship band or solo praise, including: Amazing Grace (My Chains Are Gone) • Beautiful One • Days of Elijah • Forever • In Christ Alone • Mighty to Save • Revelation Song • Sing to the King • and many more.
00311762 P/V/G...................................$21.95

7777 W. BLEMOUND RD. P.O. BOX 13819 MILWAUKEE, WI 53213

Visit Hal Leonard Online at
www.halleonard.com

0109